MEMORI
of
Eastney

As most people know, Eastney is one of the districts of Portsmouth. It is the bottom right hand corner district looking at the map. The sea is on two sides with Devonshire Avenue (although for our purposes we include Eastney Road as far as Goldsmith Avenue) being the northern boundary and Winter Road down to the beach the western one. Eastney Road and Highland Road are the main roads in the area.

Most of Eastney is a residential area, mainly for Marine and Dockyard families. On the map of 1716 Eastney was all open ground with only Eastney Farm habited. Eastney Farm was the property of John White who was a Mayor of Portsmouth. It later became the property of Lady Henderson-Durham and was sold by her in 1845. Lot 1 of this land was bought by the Crown and Eastney Barracks was erected on it.

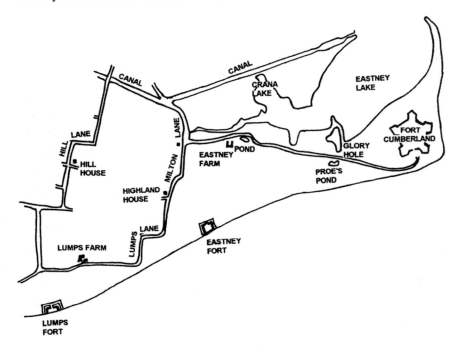

Eastney Road

Was originally Eastney Lane leading from Copnor and Milton.

Starting on the west side and going north from the junction with Highland Road.

Portsmouth Corporation Tramways Depot

The bus depot and offices were opened by the Lord Mayor, Mr F.G.Foster, on the 21st of January 1932. It was badly needed as accommodation at the North End Depot, Milton and Fratton bus sheds were strained, as was also the office accommodation at the Guildhall. The site occupied 3 acres, and the new depot allowed the repair and re-construction of tramcars and buses to be concentrated under one roof. It was divided into three sections, at the east end were the tramway running and repair sheds (later to become trolley bus sheds), at the west end was the omnibus service garage, whilst between the two were the workshops. The offices fronting Highland Road are in neo-georgian style.

The entrance/exit for trams, later trolley buses, was in Eastney Road and buses in Methuen Road. The depot was bombed on 10/11th of March 1941 and damage caused to garage and workshops and ten buses and one seafront runabout were lost by fire.

After the war a new entrance was made from Prince Albert Street and the west and east garages made into one.

The depot was used for a time by Southdown after the takeover by Portsmouth Citybus. When Southdown disposed of part of its services to Red/ Blue Admiral the use of Eastney was also transferred. The depot closed on the 27th of May 1991 on expiration of the lease from Portsmouth Corporation and the transfer of the Admirals to Hilsea.

The depot was demolished in April/May 1993. The offices are planned to be turned into a new Southsea Police Station replacing Albert Road.

"Portsmouth became a city in 1927, and buses took over from the trams. They became red and white in 1931 until 1971. The new head offices and depot in Eastney were opened in 1932. It had been planned at Bransbury Park from 1919 but the land was not suitable. In 1928 the present site was chosen to replace the other depots. The first trolleybus operated in 1934 taking tourists to the pier. The last tram stopped in 1936. The change over was expected to take ten years but was effected in two. Some buses were lent out and some destroyed in the bombing of 1941. Although the trolleybuses had extended their routes, they were replaced by buses in 1963. One man single decker buses started in 1958. Two man vehicles stopped in July 1966. Mr Ben Hall was the longest serving general manager from 1926 until 1951. Some people may have noticed his name on the side of the buses. In 1985 buses stopped using Methuen Road to enter the Depot and went in from Prince Albert Road.

Eastney Depot

"I can well remember that depot being built in 1929 and opening in 1932 after the huge steel doors had been placed in position. In the depot and in between the tram lines were inspection pits built so that electricians and mechanics could look at the underside of the trams. However, I'm sure we boys thought they had been built especially for us as we had a marvellous time racing around them much to the consternation of depot employees who used to give us a good clip around the ear when caught and this was looked upon us as one of the risks of the game! Travelling on those trams was good fun especially if one went to the upper deck, which in the majority of cases was open to the elements. One could imagine being aboard a ship and looking over the side at the pavements, the shops and the people as we passed rocking and rolling to the sway of the tram. Often the pole left the overhead wiring (from which the tram got its motive power) and would go twanging around in a circle, until the driver stopped the vehicle, and the conductor got off and drew out a very long retrieving pole from underneath the tram, and by means of a hook would regain control of the pole and replace it on the overhead wiring. It only cost a half-penny to travel from Bransbury Park to the Apollo Cinema or the King's Theatre. How well I remember going to see John Barrymore in "Rasputin the Mad Monk" at the Apollo and being taken to the King's Theatre to see Harry Welchman in the "Desert Song" where he took the part of the Red Shadow!"

"Eastney Bus Depot used to be the centre of Eastney. Once there was a pub, the Highland Arms kept by a widow with a large family. Her vegetable garden is now covered by the bus depot. The widow used to take her produce in a ponycart to Commercial Road to sell it. In about 1900, dustman's lunches were available at this pub. The dustmen on their way to the dump could get refreshment. For threepence they could get half a pint of beer, enough bread and cheese, a pickled onion and a free clay pipe. Not much profit for the widow you might think."

Eastney Gospel Mission Hall

When the Primitive Methodist iron chapel was taken down in Albert Road it was re-erected on the corner of Methuen and Eastney Roads and used by the Methodists from 1901. A Mr Norgate started using the premises in 1918 as Eastney Gospel Mission purchasing it in 1920. In 1947 plans were drawn up for a new building on the same site but due to the post war building restrictions it was decided to repair the existing church. The repairs included new corrugated iron walls and asbestos roof, new heating system and extension to the vestry and a Flextella fence surrounding the property cost just over £600. In 1962 the idea of a new building was resurrected and the sum of £8,000 was decided as the target to finance the structure. By the time the project was completed the cost had risen to around £13,000, leading to the resulting building that is to be seen today.

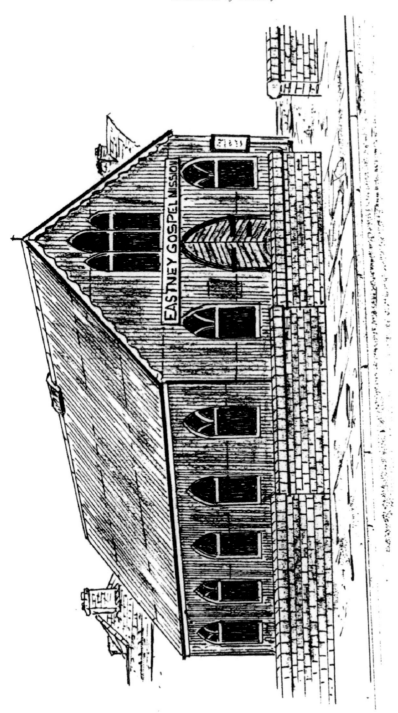

Eastney Gospel Mission

"Next door to the depot was the Mission Hall which was run under the auspices of the Norgate family, the father and two sons. The father and, I believe the eldest son lived at Portchester whilst the younger son, Gordon, lived as I recall at 16 Eastney Road opposite the Mission Hall. Every Sunday my parents sent me to that establishment to receive religious education and I had to attend morning and afternoon and sometimes in the evening also. In the summer months the Mission Hall held services at 6pm on Eastney Beach at the end of St. Georges's Road and I can well remember attending many of those meetings sitting on the edge of the promenade with the beach at least ten feet below, not as it is today level with the promenade. The services on the sea front were conducted by a lay preacher, Mr Cochrane (Harry) who lived with his wife and daughter, Eileen in number 8 Owen Street, Eastney. When we attended the actual Mission Hall on a Sunday we were issued with attendance cards and on entering the Hall these were stamped with a star or the letter L if we were late and at the end of the year book prizes were handed out in the ratio of the number of stars etc one had on the card. All in all they were good times. In the winter magic lantern shows were held once a month in the Hall on a Wednesday and they were based on such missionaries as Dr David Livingstone and General Gordon. The Mission had an excellent string orchestra which practised once a week in the Hall and any member of the congregation could join and be taught the violin for the princely sum of 2d a week. The Mission also ran a Band of Hope where its members signed a pledge not to touch the demon drink, and every year members of other Bands of Hope processed from St Mary's Recreation Ground to Alexandra Park led by various organisations drum and bugle bands! There was always a very good Christmas Party held in the Hall for we children of the congregation."

here is Methuen Road

23   Miss Olive Ballance, Physician and Surgeon

25   "My uncle and aunt, Mrs Elizabeth and Mr Alfred Chinn lived at number 25. My uncle was a kindly man, smoked a pipe and worked at St James's Hospital in the boiler room - I still possess the silver watch presented to him on his retirement! My recollections of that house are a very strong smell of Mansion polish and the very heavy tick of their old pendulum clock in their sitting room. They had one child, a boy who died in infancy, and for many years I possessed a magic lantern owned by him and which was illuminated by means of a small oil lamp. My Aunt was a strict woman with a sharp tongue and I must admit I was always scared of visiting her - although in retrospect I should imagine she was typical of her generation, i.e. Victorian and Edwardian where children should be seen but not heard."

29   R. Riches, Watch Repairer
       "He had a very large clock hanging in his front window."

35   George Atkinson, Apartments

41   William Shergold, Decorator

"There was a large plaque on his wall denoting he was the Portsmouth representative of the National Cycling Association."

here is Reginald Road

43   Walter Evans, Hairdresser

"We lads sat on a board placed across the arms of one of his chairs so that he could cut our hair without having to bend too far down!"

57   "The Johnson family lived here and I well remember one of the boys who attended Milton School with me winning a model of the Schneider Cup winner at the school raffle in 1931. I cannot recall his name but I believe it was Leslie and he went on to attend the Greenwich Naval School."

69   Mrs Annie O'Brien, Grocer

here is Landguard Road

71A   T. Jerome & Co, Wireless Engineers

71   William Flemming, Confectioner

73   "Was the residence of Mrs Scriven whose son later became an employee on the Portsmouth Trams and later in the Council offices."

75   "Was the residence of Mrs Stephens whose son went into a shoe partnership with a Mr Payne at 136 Highland Road, Eastney. With regard to Mrs Stephens, even when I knew her in the late 1920's she must have been in her 80's and she was living at that address when my father, his brothers and sister and parents were living next door. There was a standing joke in the family - the toilets in all those houses at that time were outside and could only be reached by going out the side door of the house and round to the rear of the building. Whenever a member of the family wished to use said toilet they were going outside "to see Mrs Stephens"! I'm afraid that saying is still in vogue in the family."

79   "Here lived Bill Woodward and his wife, he was an officer in the Customs & Excise."

83   "Here lived Mr Henry Moxham, his wife and family. His son Billy was a good footballer and could well have played for Pompey but for the advent of the second World War. He joined the Army and on demobilisation joined the re-constituted Portsmouth City Fire Brigade as it never returned to Police control after the war."

89   Charles Everett, Plumber

here is Westfield Road, named after the fields of Eastney.

91   Charles Spencer, Shopkeeper

"On the corner of Eastney Road with Westfield Road was the greengrocer premises of Mr Charles Spencer. My recollections of him is that he always wore black knee length gaiters as did my father when he was in his uniform of a RAC scout I can recall my mother giving me 6d to buy potatoes at his shop and because of clumsiness on my part I dropped the coin outside his shop and as "Murphy's Law" stated that if there was anything to go wrong it will go wrong, the 6d rolled down the pavement and into the gutter and into the drain outside the shop! Money in those days was scarce (as were jobs) and 6d was a lot of money when the average weekly pay was £2 to £2 10s especially when there was a family to feed. Mr Spencer suggested that my father should attend and lift up the iron drain cover, insert his arm into the drain and try and locate the missing coin! Needless to say my father declined to do that and as far as I remember we all went without vegetables that day."

97   Wilfred Veck, Confectioner
"A sweet shop run by Mrs Veck and up to the mid 70's she was still serving in that shop. One of her sons opened up a radio shop in Albert Road whilst another had a shop in Fawcett Road."

99   J. Ward & Sons, Bakers

101   Mrs K. Cuddy, Wool Stores

107   Harry Softley, junior, Fishmonger

here is Eastfield Road, named after the fields of Eastney

111   Walter Penny, Draper

113   Frank Westbrook, Butcher
"Occupied by Mr and Mrs Westbrook who ran a cooked meat shop at 115 and a pork butcher's shop at 113. At 115 of an evening there arose a delicious smell of cooked meat faggots, mushy peas, peas pudding and potatoes - I can smell and taste them now."

115   Frank Westbrook, Cooked Meat Shop

117   Harold Purse, Confectioner
"Pursey's a toy and sweet shop. Mr Pursey was rather a portly gentleman but he knew a little "gold mine" when he saw it. That shop of his was like a magnet to we children of the area. There were toys everywhere and his shop was seldom empty of envious children."

119   Sydney Maslin, Fruiterer

121   Rapid Repair Shoe Shop, Boot Repairs

125   Fort Cumberland Arms, Ernest McNie
First listed in the 1865 directory it was a Long's Brewery house.
"On the corner of Eastney Road with Devonshire Avenue was the Fort Cumberland Arms public house premises which I recall was owned in those days by Long's the brewers, unlike the Fort Cumberland Tavern opposite which was owned by Brickwoods. The Fort Cumberland Arms was a favourite with my uncles whenever they visited my grandmother and father. This public house had a large family garden where we were

taken along with our visiting cousins. I can still taste the cheese biscuits bought us to eat with our lemonade drinks or the packets of Smith's Crisps with their little blue paper bags of salt."

here is Devonshire Avenue the road named after the county was earlier known as Emery's Lane after the farming family of the area. The lane ran from Lazy Lane (Fawcett Road) to Hill Lane (Winter Road). It was split in three, becoming Manner Lane, Percy Road and Devonshire Avenue.

Regal Cinema & Café, E. Baker & Son, proprietors

Eastney Electric Theatre, was erected on the corner of Eastney Road and Devonshire Avenue and opened to the public on the 10th of October 1910. It had an outside enclosure, four exits and seated 650 on one floor. Performances were twice nightly at 6.45 and 8.45 with children's matinées on Saturdays at 1.15 and 3pm. Admission prices were 2d, 4d and 6d and for the matinées 1d, 2d and 3d. It was built, opened and furnished in three months. The hall was redecorated in 1914, re-opening on the 10th of March. The seating was re-upholstered in 1921. By 1931 the seating was increased to 829.

The cinema closed at the end of 1931 still showing silent pictures, the last in Portsmouth. It was then extended and modernised re-opening on the 3rd of February 1932 as an Atmospheric Cinema with scenes of Riviera beauty on the walls. It was known as the Regal and had continuous performances from 2.30pm. Admission prices were 7d, 9d, 1/- and 1/3d. The cinema again closed on the 24th of February 1951 for redecoration and modernisation and re-opened as the Essoldo on the 26th of March 1951. It finally closed its doors to the public on the 30th of November 1963 and was demolished to make way for shops. Up to the war a sweetshop was incorporated into the main building.

"The Eastney Electric Theatre was owned by a Mr Blake. How well I remember going there of a Saturday morning and sitting on hard wooden benches for the price of 2d to watch the silent cowboy films of early Tom Mix, and William Hart. There was a cowboy who seemed to be in every western of that period. His Stetson always had the front of it turned up against the crown of the hat and he had large drooping walrus style moustache. I can remember seeing the battle of Trafalgar being fought to the shouts and yells of we kids and to the thumping of a piano in front of the screen. On the advent of the "talkies" the cinema was all but gutted and on being rebuilt was given the name of The Regal. It was then owned by a Mr Stokes, the brother of Mr R.V.Stokes a well known Portsmouth solicitor and the commissionaire, resplendent in his blue (and sometimes red) uniform was Mr Montague as mentioned previously.

The Saturday morning children's matinées cost 3d and 4d if you sat with the elite in the back four rows. The cinema did not boast a balcony and in the evening the prices were 6d, 9d and 1/-. When there was a suitable film on it was a regular Thursday evening out to be taken there by my parents when father would ask for "two and a half nines - please." My paternal grandmother would act as baby sitter for the rest of the family until they grew old enough to accompany us. However from around 1935 it was me who became the "baby sitter" as it was deemed I could go out of an evening without a parental escort provided I was back home by 9pm and woe betide me if I wasn't back home by that time!"

137A Ernest Stride, Greengrocer
"Next door to the cinema and alongside the entrance to the cinema's car park was the greengrocery shop of Mr Stride and who later after World War II took over the shop of Mr Albion on the corner of Eastfield Road."

137 J. Young & Sons, Fried Fish Shop
"Next door again was the fried fish shop of Mr Young. The back entrance of that shop led into the car park of the cinema and there was always a strong smell of stale fish coming from his dustbins left outside his back door."

"Number 137 (175?- Editor) Eastney Road was a hobby shop owned I think by a Mr Mould from which he sold 3 ply wood for fret work, fret work saw blades, plans for model making etc. It was from that shop that my father bought the material for the cabinet he made for his new wireless."

139 John Parsons, Decorator

141 Charles Cooper & Sons, Butchers

143 Charles Burton, Boot Maker

145 Herbert Woods, Clothier

147 Mrs Marion Green, Tobacconist
"Green's the tobacconist and newsagent outside of which we lads often stopped to take a quick look through the comics hung up outside the shop until chased away by the owner."

149 Walter Thomas, Grocer
"On the corner of Suffolk Road was a grocer whose name now escapes me but his shop was in later years taken over by Mr J.Arkell, the chemist and a dentist on the upper floor. On Mr Arkell's death the shop became part of the Tremlett group of Chemists."

here is Suffolk Road the road is named after the county

151 Miss Elsie Langer, Shopkeeper and Post Office
"A Post Office cum sweet shop, card and toy shop which in my day was run by Mrs Langer and then in the thirties the Hilder family."

153 Dittman & Malpas Ltd, Corn Merchants
"Was a corn and seed shop which later became one of the chain of shops

owned by Dittman And Malpas."
155 Thomas Brackpool, Confectioner
157 Frederick Viney, Confectioner and Pastrycook
"Was a cake shop and I remember buying crumpets there in the winter months for a farthing each."
159 William Moore, Ironmonger
"A shop about which my brother and sisters still talk, Mr Moore, the ironmonger. When the family kettles sprang a leak then I would be sent to his shop to buy a kettle patch. This was in reality two pieces of tin plate about the size of a florin with a small nut and bolt running through its middle. One piece of plate was placed on one side of the hole causing the leak and the remaining piece on the other side. The small bolt was then passed through the holes which had been lined up and with the nut, the bolt would be tightened up thereby securing the leak. His shop was full of cooking utensils of all shapes and sizes on shelves, on the floor and even hanging from the shop ceiling. One had to step over utensils when walking around his shop."
167 Portsea Island Mutual Co-Operative Society Ltd, Grocers
"The counters had marble tops and there were chairs for the customers to sit on. Your money was delivered to the cashier by an overhead wire system and food bought was wrapped in brown paper parcels. Broken biscuits were very popular and the biscuits were sold loose from boxes covered with glass."

here is Middlesex Road the road is named after the county.
169 Portsmouth Fruit & Flower Stores, A. Dannan and B. Cobell, proprietors
171 Thomas Lindfield, Draper
"Lindfield's, the drapers. I was often dragged in there by my mother when she bought lace, elastic and cottons as she was a dab hand at making dresses for my two sisters or altering clothing to fit my brother or myself - that of course was a sign of those times when the majority of mothers knew how to handle a needle and thread."
173 W & R Fletcher Ltd, Butchers
"Fletcher's the butchers who also had a shop in Highland Road. I can always remember his beef sausages as being dark red in colour and selling at 6d a pound."
175 Sidney Mould, Provision Dealer
177 Godding & Son, Stationers
179 James Smith, Fishmonger
"Was the shop of Mr Curtis who sold wet fish and was a favourite place for the Langstone Harbour fishermen to sell their catches."
181 George Gilbert, Confectioner
"George Gilbert who ran the sweet shop, his son now runs the same shop.

During World War II George joined the Auxiliary Fire Service in Portsmouth and served his time in Portsmouth. He remembered me well when I introduced myself to him when I was a cadet at the Central Fire Station. We became firm friends when after the war I returned to the City Police and was stationed at Eastney Police Station. He sold really lovely ice-cream from a tub outside his shop when we were lads."

183   Richard Tribe, Fruiterer

185   Howard Jeans, Hardware Merchant

187   Albert Stewart, Confectioner

"Another sweet shop, Stewarts. We lads always found him to be rather grumpy and his shop was not one of those which we lads of the area attended often."

189   Bray's Ltd, Chemists

"On the corner of Essex Road was Brays, the chemist and it was from that shop, much to the annoyance of my father, I used to purchase lengths of old 35mm film for a copper or so and make stink bombs from it. Ah! happy days!!"

here is Essex Road the road is named after the county.

Eastney Police Station

"The Police Station, during the 1920 as an economy measure, was closed for a few years and it became the residence of P.C. Tom Lincoln until public pressure caused it to be reopened. In later years, during the 1940's and possibly the early 1950's P.C. Lincoln drove the forces "Black Maria" from the Magistrates Court, then in Western Parade, to Winchester Prison with persons who had been sentenced by the court and also to convey prisoners from the City's Police stations to the court."

Eastney Fire Station

Old White House, George Collins

First listed in 1867 as the White House, by 1879 it had changed to the Old White House.

here is Goldsmith Avenue, named after the Goldsmith family.

Returning on the east side were ....

footpath that marks the northern side of the canal.

Milton Park Garage Co Ltd

here is Old Canal, another footpath on the southern side of the canal that leads to a road called Old Canal.

Council School

"The teachers were Miss Rose, Miss Sketch (the girls used to tease her about her boyfriend in the Navy), Miss Murray, Miss Packer and Miss Hearst. Miss Shaw was the headmistress she wore her hair in a bun. She married the curate of St Cuthbert's Church. When she married she left and Miss Robson took over. Mr Mansell was the caretaker. Cooking was held at Reginald Road School and laundry at Meon Road."

here is Dunbar Road
168   Bendell & White, Haulage Contractors
166   Osborne Stores Ltd, Provision Merchants
164   Harry Stanford, Chiropodist
162   Walter Evans, Hairdresser
160   William Peace, Fried Fish Shop

here is Kingsley Road
158   W. Pink & Sons Ltd, Grocers
156   Chapman's Laundry, Receiving Office
154   Walter Strevens, Draper
152   William Banting & Son, Butchers
142   John Harris, Dairyman

here is Glasgow Road
140   Lloyds Bank Ltd
134   Arthur Berry, Apartments
Bransbury Recreation Ground

here is Bransbury Road which takes its name from Bransbury Farm which in turn was named after the family that farmed there.
130   Fort Cumberland Tavern, Charles Hurdle
      First listed in the 1865 directory. It was a Blake's Gosport Ale House becoming Brickwoods. The pub closed in 1989 and has since been converted into flats.
      "On the corner of Bransbury with Eastney Road was the world famous "Hurdles" pub. In those days the licensee was Mr James Charles Hurdle and on his death his wife took over the licence. I cannot remember much about James Charles but I well remember his wife. I can picture her still, dressed in a long black Edwardian type dress which covered her from throat to foot, wearing calf length boots and with her hair tied back into a bun. The pub was of course the Fort Cumberland Tavern and on her death, a son Charles took over the licence and he later became president of the Portsmouth Licensed Victuallers Association. During the second world war his pub became known to thousands of servicemen of all nationalities stationed in the city. Another son took over the very large garage at 110 Eastney Road, a few doors away from the pub and it was here that I had to go twice a week with our radio's accumulator to have it charged."

120   L. Cotrell, Carpenter

118   George Bastard, Coal Dealer

114-116   Austin's, Timber Merchants

110-112   Hurdle's Garage

108   "Next door at number 108 lived Dr John Liston, a surgeon who later opened a surgery just inside Devonshire Avenue but later left medicine for the knife at the Royal Portsmouth Hospital. It was he who set my arm when I broke it."

between 106 and 108 was the Mission of the Holy Cross or St Cross Mission Hall which has since been demolished.

"There was a large open space next to Dr Liston's house which belonged to St James's Church and which was used as an allotment but also contained St Cross Mission Hall, a part of the parish of St James's Church although more often than not it was never used as a Mission Hall but kept closed."

104   William Hastings, House Decorator

98   "Here lived Mrs Dorothy Woods who as Dorothy Butt lived with her brother Leslie and parents at 46 Eastney Road and went to school with my mother. In the 30's Leslie Butt became a carpenter with Handley's of Southsea, and during the second world war he joined the Auxiliary Fire Service and served in the carpenter's shop at the Central Fire Station as well as carrying out his normal fire duties."

88   Arthur Wernham, Fruiterer

86   Cyril Moir, Hair Dresser

84   James Green, Herbalist

"Mr Green, the herbalist where for a ½d we could buy ginger candy, whilst next door was a sweetshop called the Blue Bird."

82   Miss L Bird, Confectioner

72   Charles Riley, Fried Fish Dealer

68   Ernest Hithersay, Boot Repairer

"Mr Ern Hithersay, a boot and shoe repairer who joined the Special Constabulary at the outbreak of the second world war and in which he served throughout, retiring to Cornwall after the war to open a small guest house."

66   Mrs Ethel Taylor, Cooked Meats

64   Mrs Beatrice Stevens, Baby Linen

62   Harry Carr, Florist

60   John Arkell, Chemist

"Most families relied on their local chemist and ours for the Eastney District was Mr J.Arkell. I can see him now, a tall rather thin and gaunt looking man peering at us over his glasses. He was a well-liked and kindly individual who certainly knew his medicines. In the early 50's he moved his premises to the corner of Suffolk and Eastney Roads on the opposite corner to the Post Office."

58	Mrs Alice Wakely, Corndealer
56	Mrs C. Brock, Newsagent

"The newsagents was run by Mrs Brock and her two daughters one of whom married Jimmie Allen the Portsmouth, Aston Villa and England centre half and who, in later years due to a severe leg injury retired to become mine host at the Festing Hotel, Highland Road."

54	Reginald Perkins, Shopkeeper
52	Mrs E. Stratton, Apartments
44	Richard Parker, Tailor
40	Mrs F. Gifford, Apartments
36	Mrs Osmond, Apartments
34	Herbert Sidey, Plumber
18	Henry Phillips, Gents' Hairdresser
12-14	Mrs Elizabeth Chapman, Draper

"Mrs Chapman who ran a clothing/drapery shop at that address. She had two children, a boy and a girl. Both of whom attended Milton School and I always recall them being dressed in their Scottish tartans to participate in the Empire Day scenarios put on at the school to commemorate that day."

4	Henry Softley, Fishmonger

"The Softley family ran a wet fish shop. I am afraid the head of that family, Henry was a great man for the bottle and often had to be taken home from the Fort Cumberland Arms singing merrily on his way - I went to school with his son as I did with the son of Cameron's who lived next door at number 6."

2	John Harrison, Beer Retailer

First known as the World's End according to the Evening News by 1887 it had become the Barrack Cellar. Standing on the corner with Henderson Road until 1972 when it was demolished.

Highland Road

Named simply because the lane that was here in early days was one of the high points on the neighbourhood.
Starting on the north side from the junction with Albert Road

3	Walter Simons, Fruiterer
5-7	William Churchill, Stationer
9-11	Smith & Vosper Ltd, Bakers

One of the many branches of the well known chain.

here is St Augustine Road

13	Thomas Eeles, Confectioner

Barrack Cellars

15   Harry Parker, Greengrocer
17-19 Martin Phillips, Grocer
21   Alfred Sherwood, Boot maker
23   Charles Newton, Outfitter
25   John Marsh, Butcher
27   George Guttridge, Woolshop
29   Benjamin Gregory, Stationer
31   Uwantus, Dyers & Cleaners
33   George Putnam, Boot Maker
35   John Alderson, Tobacconist
37   Southern Products, Wireless Engineers
39   James Savage, Fried Fish Shop
39   Burgoyne, Baker & Co, monumental masons

here is Brompton Road
41   Frederick Norton, Florists
43   H. Woodruff & Co., Tobacconists
45   Arthur Burridge, Fishmonger
47   Edgar Allan, Draper
49   William Smith , Corn Merchant
51-55 Seal, Cycle agent
57   Batchelor & Putman's Bakeries Ltd. One of the branches of the less
        well known local firms.
59   William Lasseter, Boot maker
61   Edward Williams & Co., Gents' Outfitters
63   Charles Handley, Confectioner
67   Young Bros, Monumental masons
        Later Seal Bros, Motor Showroom

here is Haslemere Road
St Margaret's Church.
        Opened in 1899 as a prefab church dedicated by the Bishop of Southampton
        on the 21st of October. The permanent building was commenced in 1902,
        the architect was J.T.Lee of London. The new church was built around
        the old iron church as can be seen in a postcard on display in the City
        Museum and Art Gallery. The church was left with a temporary east wall
        which was not replaced until 1965. A new institute to replace the old St
        Columba's Hall was built alongside.
        "The parish church of Eastney is St Margaret of Scotland. This is
        apparently because there was a mission hall of St Columba, in which
        were two paintings of St Columba and St Margaret. Now in St Columba's
        chapel are two statues of these saints, carved from lime wood.
        Small congregations meet there, particularly the elderly when its cold. St

Margaret was the wife of Malcolm III and daughter of King Henry of England. One of her children, David, was noted for his good works, the same as his mother. The church has taken a long time to grow upon the previous waste ground, in the style of simplified redbrick gothic. The foundation stone was laid in 1902 and the church consecrated by the Bishop of Winchester in 1903. The original plans show an elaborate main entrance but lack of money meant this didn't happen. Various parts have been added when possible. The church is actually built back to front, that is, it faces west. When I went there in 1950 there were chairs, now there are pews. A large chair or cathedra awaits the Bishop of Portsmouth when he visits. The white stone screens were added as a memorial to Martin Phillips who was killed in 1917. The shiny brass lectern is an eye catching sight. The large circular window was added in 1960, this was designed by Christopher Webb a noted expert in this field. The baldachino had to be lowered to accommodate it. Mr J.Cowan played the large organ for fifty years. This was a gift from the famous benefactor Andrew Carnegie. The church has been spared war damage, but in 1941 a fire at a nearby furniture store threatened it. The store was gutted but a changing wind saved the church as it was being cleared.

The first vicar was William King 1899-1903, he was followed until 1918 by Robert Thorley. In 1934 Philip Baker took over, followed by Allan Hill in 1943. He was succeeded by Ronald Scruby in 1958 and Harry Gilroy in 1965. Next was Peter Law followed by the present vicar Peter Kelly. The original vicarage has disappeared and the vicar has to live some distance away.

The post war church caters for a large, varied crowd of people. Apart from the Scout and Guide groups etc. a dramatic society stages regular shows and pantomimes."

here is Highland Terrace

97   Beer Retailer. Listed as the Victoria Arms in 1887 and The Victoria in 1901. It is then unnamed in the directories until 1958 when it is the Victoria Arms. 1960 finds the first reference in the directories to the Grave Diggers. It was one of Young's Brewery tied houses. In 1980 it was briefly known as Diggers but soon reverted back to the old name.

here is White Cloud Place, named after battle of White Cloud Mountain which involved the Marines.

99   Alexander Chamberlain, Watchmaker
101   Dr Henry Wingate Maltby, Physician & Surgeon
103   Smeed & Smeed, off licence
105   Mrs A Cass, Stationer
107   Leonard Brown, Grocer

109   Miss Agnes Turner, Shopkeeper
111-113   Edgar Allan, Draper
Eastney Gospel Room
     Listed here from 1923 to 1928, now McCullums timber merchants
117   Arthur Eaton, Butcher

here is Winter Road, this was previously one of the old lanes of the area, Hill Lane. Hill lane ran along the line of Priory Crescent and Winter Road, although the southern end emerged where Haslemere Road is now. It was named after one of the farming families of Portsmouth. It was renamed after another Portsmouth family.
119   Ward & Sons, Bakers
     A branch of the well known city firm.
121   Ernest Shervell, Ellectrical Engineer
123   George Morgan, Confectioner
125   Mrs Dorothy Cooper, Milliner
127   John Holmes, Hairdresser
129   Charles Hayden, Photographer
131-141   is a terrace of shops known as The Broadway built in 1906.
131-133   Arthur Bull Ltd, China and Glass warehouse
135   G.A.Cooper, Butcher
137   Walter Stevens, Tobacconist
139   Osborne Stores Ltd., Provision Merchants
141   Timothy White Co. Ltd., Chemists.
     A branch of the well known city firm.

here is Clegg Road
143   Boots, Chemists
145   Mrs Helen Riches, Outfitter
147   Thomas Still, Fruiterer
149   Ernest Keene, Stationer
151   Maypole Dairy Co. Ltd.
153   World's Stores Ltd
155   Francis & Son, Butchers
157   Thomas Till & Sons, Bakers
159   George Corbin, Boot maker
161   Herbert Woods & Co, Drapers
163-165   David Minter, Outfitter

here is Hellyer Road
167-169   Leslie Hapgood, Gents' Outfitter
171   Sydney Lewis, Furniture Dealer
173   Gilham Brothers Ltd., Fruiterers

175   W & H Couzens, Laundries
177   Pearks' Dairies Ltd., Grocers
179   Joseph Frisby Ltd., Boot Makers
181   George Peters & Co. Ltd., Wine & Spirit Merchants
183   Frederick Norton & Son, Florists (Nurseries)
Here is a terrace of three buildings Alma Terrace
1   Lloyds Bank Ltd.
2   Hayling Island Egg Producers Ltd.
3   Charles Cotton, Butchers
193   Alma Arms
The public house is first listed in the 1864 directory. It was named after the Crimean War battle site.
201   Southsea Laundry Co. Limited
203   Leethems (Twilfit) Ltd., Corset Makers
Here is a terrace Alexandra Terrace
217 (1)   Mrs Alice Ross, Newsagent
219 (2)   Brown, Builder
221 (3)   King & King, Butchers
223 (4)   Frederick Hilliard, Draper

here is Alma Terrace
Here is a terrace of six Spithead View
225 (1)   Stanley Ballard, Tobacconist
227 (2)   Arthut Sweeney, Fried fish shop
229 (3)   Mrs Florence Matthews, Grocer
231 (4)   Mrs Francis Wheavil, Shopkeeper
233 (5)   Arthur Mellish, Fruiterer
235 (6)   Mrs Baillie-Hamilton, Confectioner
237   Jack Laddie, Draper
239   Joseph Baits, Boot maker

here is Prince Albert Street the street was named after Queen Victoria's husband.

Earlier on one corner of Prince Albert Street was the Marine Artillery Arms first listed in 1874. From the following year the directories refer to the pub as the Royal Marine Artillery Arms. It closed in 1916
241   H Shimbart, Grocer
243   Frederick Hilliard, Clothier
Was earlier Kent & Sons, Drapers
"Was a place of fascination on account of the pulley system they had for taking your cash. Your money was put into a container which was then screwed into the overhead runner and it went whizzing across the shop to the office, and presently back would come your change. Prices were

usually so much and elevenpence three farthings and they always gave you a few pins instead of farthings change."

245	William Toms, Fishmonger
249	W & R Fletcher Ltd, Butchers
251	F.G.Currey, Pork butcher
253	Toms, Fried Fish Shop
255	A.M.Steel, Timber & Builders' Merchant

Here are two cottages The Elms

259 (2)   John Tindall, Confectioner
261(1)   James Bruce & Son, Dairymen

Here are two cottages King's Cottages
Here is a terrace of four, Cambridge Terrace

281 (3)   Sidney Cleverley, Hairdresser
283-285 (1-2)   John Fulljames, Pawnbroker
287   Frederick Radcliffe, Corn merchant
289   Ernest Simmons, Greengrocer
291   Welcome Home Dining Rooms, F.H.Ruffles
295-297   Beer Retailer
        The Mayflower dates back to 1865 when it is listed as a beer retailer. First named in 1887. It was a Long's House
299   Highland Arms
        First listed in 1898 as a beer retailer, named in 1923. The pub closed in 1984 and has since been converted into offices.

here is Eastney Road
Returning on the south side

182   Clement Bros (Portsmouth) Ltd., Coal Merchants Office
180   Eastney Garage, John Fox
178   John Fox, Refreshment Rooms
176   Mrs Winifred Marriner, Confectioner
174   James Chandler, Coal merchant
172   Mrs M Roulston, Fancy Repository
        "This was a veritable Aladdin's Cave of almost everything from the proverbial pin to an elephant. Here, a man could buy his wife a pair of vases to placate her when he came home 'three sheets to the wind' or a wife could go and get remedies for various ills, for Mrs Roulston was a dab hand at concocting potions from her variety of drugs. She also sold sweets, toys and bric-a-brac of every kind and one could spend hours just looking in the window."
170   Arthur Churcher, Grocer
168   Thomas Hallett, Ham & Beef Dealer
166   William Marsh, Butcher
164   T Powell, Confectioner

Map

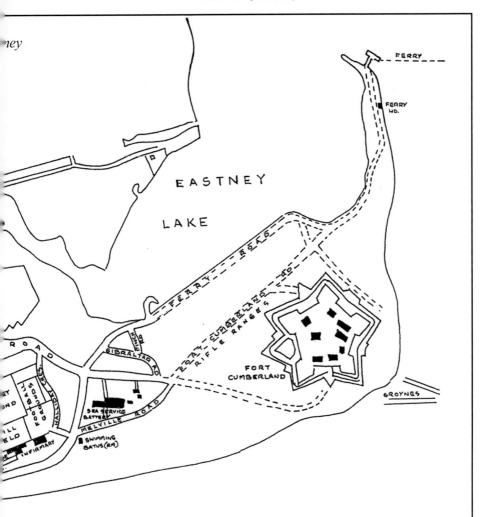

EASTNEY CIRCA 1958

—— — —— BOUNDARY AS PER BOOK

158   Hoar & Dumbrill Ltd., Dairy
Was earlier Waterman's, Dairy
"Mrs Waterman's Dairy with its black and white chequered floor and great brass churns. Here we came with a small lidded can for half a pint of milk, or a quarter of butter if your mother could afford it."

156-154   E.H.Butler, Cycle Depot and Wireless Dealers

here are Kassassin Street and Eastney Street

152   Beer Retailer, known as the Cambridge Arms from 1874 to 1976 when it was renamed the Sirloin of Beef. The original name perhaps coming with the Marines who were stationed in the Clarence Barracks near the Cambridge Barracks for a time.

150   Bertie Gibbon, Tobacconist

148   Mrs Lily Hill, Confectioner

146   Miss E Woods, Draper

144   Arthur Tuppen, Picture Frame maker

142   William Nutter, Newsagent

140   William Sharpe, Stationer and Post Office

138   Payne & Stevens, Boot dealer

136   Radio Electric Supplies, George Smith

134   Mrs K Steel, Ironmonger
"He and his brothers were pillars of the Wesleyan Chapel on the corner of Adair Road and all his daughters were Sunday School Teachers. Most of the children in the area went to the Wesleyan Sunday School and every summer, five or six charabancs would take them for the day to Redhill or Rowlands Castle. There was also Good Friday tea when you took your own mug and they gave you hot cross buns. Simple enough treats but something the children looked forward to all year."

132   C.Knight & Son, Bakers
"His bakery was in Adair Road and if you looked in on your way home from school, you could watch him icing cakes and perhaps get a squirt of icing in your mouth."

130   William Lockhart, Grocer
"Kept by Mr Lockhart and his brother. There was no self service in those days, you waited whilst the bacon was sliced and the tea and currants etc., weighed and put into paper 'pokes'."

here is Adair Road, named after a Marine Major General.

Victoria Wesleyan Church
In 1867 Sarah Robinson purchased a plot of land in order to develop a home similar to the Royal Sailor's Rest for Marines to spend their time. She purchased more land in 1877 but then sold it to the Methodists for a soldier's home. The foundation stone of the Victoria Soldier's Home was

laid in July 1885 and the home opened in 1886. It was enlarged several times. The hall alongside, the Victoria Hall opened on the 8th of September 1886 and still stands as the hall for Eastney Methodist Central Hall which was built in 1928 on the site of the institute.

here is Priory Road

122   Arthur Jeans, Chemist
120   William Luxton, Butcher
118   J.Fitzpatrick, Greengrocer
116   Thomas Langley, Cooked Meats
114   Gerald Turner, Confectioner
112   Frederick Keeping, Greengrocer
110   Beer Retailer, First listed as the Royal Oak from 1887 to 1895. It is next named from 1958 to 1977 as the Three Marines. It was a Jewell's Brewery house.

here is Highland Street. At one time a wall separated this Street from the continuation known as Morley Road. This was reputedly because of landowner Lady Morley. The wall has since been removed.

In this street was the Eastney Methodist Church built in 1866. They transferred to the Highland Road building in 1889 and for a while the building was used as a hall for St Columba's Church.

108   Beer Retailer
      First listed in 1887 as the Highland House it closed during the sixties and is now a private house. It was tied to Mew Langton's Brewery.
100   John Reeve, Corn Dealer
96   Hills & Son, Fishmonger
94   E Stokes & Son, Wireless Supplies

here is Owen Street

      Named after Thomas Owen the local architect and developer of Southsea. He also bought land in this area and perhaps would have developed Eastney in a similar manner to Southsea had he not died.

St Columba's Hall

      Built in 1885 in red brick, to replace an earlier prefab church, the architect was J.H.Ball. It was transferred to St Margaret's in 1889 and used as the hall for St Margaret's Church until it was sold around 1948. The building survives as part of a wood shop.

90   Percy Wheavil, Hairdresser
88   Brown, builders' workshop
84   Charles Leetham & Co, Blouse manufacturers

here is Ward Road, named after the Plaintiff in the Highland Cemetery Case.

82   Mrs L.M.Bray, Apartments
76   Dashwood & Sons (Original Firm), Undertakers

here is Wainscott Road
74   John Druce, Leather Merchant
70   George Harding, Wardrobe Dealer
66   Henry Henderson, Fish Restaurant
64   William Vallor, Fruiterer
62   Portsea Island Mutual Co-operative Society, Grocers

here is Kimberley Road, named after the battle.
60   W.Pink & Sons Ltd, Grocers
58   Fred Penny, Hairdresser
56   Mrs Nellie Harris, Confectioner
Highland Road Cemetery
        The pub near the main gate has a most suitable name of the Gravediggers Arms. Many people from different walks of life have come to rest in the cemetery since its opening in 1854. Some people have been well known. Monsignor John Vertue as the first Roman Catholic Bishop of Portsmouth buried in 1890. Rev, later Canon, John Horan in 1885. He wanted to build a Catholic Cathedral next to the Theatre Royal but it was an unsuitable site. Msgr John Crookall was first provost 1887. The Dagastino family has been here since 1919 and Brickwoods from 1894. Charles Tomkins, first vicar of St Pauls 1903,

Highland Road Cemetery

Johnathan Gain paymaster RN 1861 and family, Dr John Miller, Insp Gen Army Hospitals 1873, the Dupree family have their own mausoleum. W. Dupree 1st Baronet and Lord Mayor and eleven of his family are there. The Charpentier family 1880 were guide book publishers. William Treadgold and family, engineers. Mr John Russell 1884 was keeper of the Royal Apartments on the Victoria & Albert Royal Yacht. Col Rowland Richardson 1900 76th Regiment, a veteran of the Afghan Campaign. Rev J.C.Leichman, wife and child died in sea collision on the Oceana 1912. Mr Walter Hooper was killed falling in HMS Research 1865. Mr Loius Van De Bergh was the Dutch Consul in Portsmouth 1872 holder of the Lion Legion of Honour and Red Eagle of Prussia. Col Hugh Cochrane V.C. Royal Fusiliers buried 1884, the tombstone states 'A True Highlander'. Other V.C.s in the cemetery are Rear Admiral Raby, Vice Admiral Hewett, Israel Harding, John Robarts, Hugh Shaw and William Temple.

here is Bristol Road, named after city

54	Fay & Son, Decorators
52	Geer, Florist
50	Fraser & White Ltd., Coal Merchants
48	Frederick Braby, Hairdresser
44	Wesley Miller, Dentist
40	Claude Voller, Estate Agent

here is Andover Road, named after the town

20	Bray's Ltd., Chemists

here is Exeter Road, named after City

18	W.Burden, Grocer
16	Percy Snook, Confectioner
14	The Central Library, Thomas Davies
12	Wilson Sinclair, Provision Merchant
10	Post Office & Telegraph Office, Mrs Sandford
8	Walter Swanton, Outfitter
6	Edward Mariner, Stationer
4	George Gutteridge, Wool Stores

Festing Hotel

A large public house on the corner with Festing Grove. Built in 1896 to the designs of A.H.Bone. It is named after a Commandant of the Marines.

Eastney Beach

"When I was a small boy I remember going to Eastney Beach, although I lived in Petworth Road on the Milton/Copnor border. My mother had come from Peterborough which is in Cambridgeshire now. She met my father there. My father came from Rochdale, Lancashire and they both arrived in Portsmouth. Most of my relations lived in and around Peterborough. Before World War II some of them would visit us for a seaside holiday. My grandfather and grandmother, two or more aunts, uncles and cousins would arrive by train. They would bring strange food like haslet and faggots. When the young ones went to bed, tired with the journey, the older ones would catch up on the gossip. The tongues would wag until the early hours. Eastney beach was a popular destination. The toddlers would be in pushchairs with bags of food and toys hanging on. Everyone would start the trek happily. We went out the back door, through the alleys across Romsey Avenue into Eastern Road. There were allotments on the corner of Eastern and Langstone Roads then. We came out of a gate at the extremity of Milton Cemetery, along Velder Avenue, past the Good Companion turning into Euston Road, Hollam Road, Locksway Road, Eastney Road and Henderson Road. Sometimes we would pass the Marine Barracks and Swimming Baths or sometimes through the back streets past the Pumping Station and near Fort Cumberland. We spent many days on Eastney Beach. It was only pebbles and still is, but it was not so crowded as Southsea Beach. One day we found a picnic basket. Sadly, there was no food left, only plates and cutlery. "

Anton Cox

"I remember going to Eastney Beach back in the late 20's. We used to go from our house in Malins Road, Buckland. I had several brothers and sisters, so with our parents we set off for a day out. We liked Eastney Beach because there was some sand there then. My father owned a tent which was usually locked away near the beach. My brothers and I went ahead to erect the tent, and the others followed with the food and drink. We all enjoyed our days on the beach"

Charlie Renyard

Fort Cumberland

The original Fort Cumberland was a star shaped fort built in 1746, by the Duke Of Cumberland. It was replaced by the existing fort in 1786 by the Duke of Richmond. It was built by convict labour who had to be marched all the way from the Dockyard, later they were housed on hulks in Eastney Lake. It features some early prefabricated parts - such as the cast iron door frames. The two landward bastions are still in their original state apart from some bomb damage. Its purpose was to control the Langstone Harbour entrance. Built in a

Large Gun – Eastney Barracks

pentagonal shape with arrowhead salients at each angle, a dry moat with a ravelin on the west side. The parapets are brick with stone faced ramparts. Ringing the fort behind the ramparts are vaulted brick chambers.

This fortress is the most important surviving example in Britain, last used in World War II and now closed to the public.

There were also two other forts to protect the eastern approaches, Eastney Forts east and west. These were linked by a passage but only part of it remains. One of the forts has been modified and is used as a radar station.

For many years there was a large rifled gun on the foreshore in front of the fort but it disappeared around the time of the Second World War presumably as scrap.

"Next to Fort Cumberland is the more visible Fraser Gunnery Range. The 100 foot lattice towers are a landmark for miles. It is situated right on the promenade of Eastney Beach or rather where the promenade should be. The approach road is at the back, connecting with Fort Cumberland Road. The establishment started about 1930 to test large naval guns firing out to sea. The warning signs are still there although the guns are gone. After World War II the site became HMS St George. Its purpose was to train sailors to become officers, a special duties school. For the last few years it has been an Admiralty Radar Establishment as the radar scanner on the tallest tower will show. How many men have passed through here in its time?"

In 1836-9 the C-In-C Portsmouth was Rear Admiral Sir Philip Durham. His wife, Ann Henderson, sold Eastney Farm, and some of Milton, about 50 acres to the War Dept. It had previously been owned by the White family of Southwick. Eastney Barracks was started in 1858 and completed in 1867. It was built on the site of a small fort with a three sided courtyard and open to the sea. Made in a classical tradition with brown and red brick. The Officers mess is Jacobean style on a first floor level, with stone facing.

"I went to school in Eastney Barracks, as did most of the children who lived in houses adjacent to the barracks. Only children whose fathers were serving in the armed forces were allowed to go to the Barrack School. My father was in the Royal Navy but my mother's family were all Royal Marine Artillery as it was then, indeed her father was Drum-Major of the regiment for many years and she lived in the barracks, where in those days there were married quarters. I have a certificate signed by the Colonel Commandant giving my grandfather permission to marry and vouching for the respectability of his prospective bride! He also agreed to a small sum being deducted from his weekly pay, (it was called living in money) so his wife could have a doctor and midwife in attendance when she had their children.

I was born in Worsley Street near enough to the sea to hear the waves lapping on shingle on still, winter nights. The houses were small two up and two down and a scullery, with the privvy at the bottom of the garden, but we all seemed quite content and the rent was only four shillings a week (20p). In rough weather and at high tide the sea would come right up St Georges Road and I remember one winter it came up outside our door and the boys were fishing out of the bedroom windows with a bent pin and piece of string."

The Royal Marines

King Charles II had raised a special regiment in 1664 for sea service. This was known as The Duke of York and Albany's Maritime Regiment of Foot. The Duke of York was Governor of Portsmouth then. Later he became King James II. In 1755 another war with France and Spain caused fifty companies of Marines to be raised. There were twelve at Chatham, eighteen at Plymouth and twenty in Portsmouth. These divisions were known as the Grand Divisions, the framework of the Marines for the next 200 years. The Portsmouth Division was originally at Hilsea. In 1755 about 1,000 officers and men were moved into billets in the town. By 1783 Marines began garrison duty in the Dockyard. Kings Cooperage and brewery in St Nicholas Street was converted into Clarence Barracks. In 1802 the First Sea Lord, Lord St. Vincent suggested to King George III that they be Royal Marines. They became the Royal Marines Light Infantry. Two years later, one division became the Royal Marines Artillery. The Duke of Clarence presented their new colours on Southsea Common on 27th October 1827. The RMLI moved to Forton Barracks, Gosport, in 1848. The RMA took over premises in the High Street and St Thomas Street for the officers. The men were divided between Gunwharf and Fort Cumberland. Later they all moved to Fort Cumberland. The RMA was made a 3,000 strong division on the 1st November 1859. The newly built Eastney Barracks was opened in 1867. In 1871 the Marines outnumbered the civilians, being 1,162 servicemen. Still in 1879 RMA Officers were travelling between Fort Cumberland and Gunwharf. In 1923 the RMLI, known as the Red Marines left Forton Barracks and came to Eastney Barracks. Their own barracks were falling down. They joined the RMA, the Blues, becoming The Royal Marines. Sadly after all these years the Marines have left Eastney Barracks. HMS Nelson is now the home of the Marine Band which started in 1763.

The first permanent garrison was established in 1775. Originally stationed in inns, ale houses their first real barracks was Clarence Barracks in 1765. The first reference to the RMA is in 1817 on exercise at Fort Cumberland. In 1859 it was decided that the RMA should reside at Fort Cumberland and 16 companies were raised. Building of Eastney Barracks commenced in 1862. The water tower was added in 1871. The clocks from Woolwich Dockyard were added later. In 1927? the School of Music left for Deal, in Kent.

The Marines had their own church. The first church was known as the Crinoline Church and stood on ground to the south of the sharp bend in Cromwell Road by the Eastney Tavern. The site is marked by a mushroom shaped stone which can be glimpsed when the hedges around it allow. It was originally a mobile field hospital used in the Crimean War and was shipped back to Portsmouth and served as a temporary church for St Simon's and St Bartholomew's before being moved here in 1864. It was a circular (twenty sided) wooden building. The permanent church, St Andrew's, was built in Henderson Road in 1904/5 after the Princess of Wales laid the foundation stone on the 16th of March 1904. It was closed in 1973 but still in use in 1990 as a rehearsal room for the band.

"I decided to become a Marine because it was better than being a farm labourer. My uncle was a Marine also. Because my name is Lewis they said I was a 'Taffy'. My home was Pimlico, a village in Northants not Wales, but the name stuck. I joined in 1921 when we were the Royal Marine Light Infantry, the Red marines. All in all it was a good life because I stayed 25 years. I lived in Eastney Barracks from time to time. We were sent to ships, did our time, came back, had leave and a few weeks later went off on another ship. I served on several ships - The Iron Duke, Warspite, Royal Oak, Barham and others. As befitting a Marine, I learnt a lot about guns, eventually becoming an armourer. For two years I was a gunnery instructor at Fort Cumberland. I've travelled the world - Norway, China, East Indies, Meditterranean, New Zealand, etc. I played football for the Marines as well. When World War II finished, I left to settle down. The Dockyard was my life for several years as an engine fitter, until I retired at 65. Now at 88 I live quietly with my memories."

Harold 'Taffy' Lewis

The Glory Hole

"The Glory Hole situated at the southern end of Hayling Ferry Road was just a vast stretch of water. The contract for filling in this hole was awarded to a transport firm named Parks of Portsmouth. They had a fleet of steam Foden tractors, to drive these the driver steered and the mate had to change gear. They were similar to the old fairground tractors with very large driving wheels at the back. I think that there were 4 or 5 of these tractors that were used for transporting the waste material from the Dockyard. I myself was a mate on one of these tractors for a while so I do know about the workings of the job and what we carried.

When I knew that the Corporation were going to build houses on the Glory Hole, I for one knew they were evading the truth, because the material that came out of the Dockyard consisted of Asbestos and metal. In the time it took to fill the hole, I would say approximately 25 years, there must have been hundreds of tons of these materials. So when the council said that it was perfectly safe to build houses I knew they were wrong."

"Still at the Glory Hole there used to be a very large mock up of a twin barrelled gun. It used to stand on the corner of Melville Road opposite the condemned houses. I think it was called Big Bertha, but I can't be sure of its name."

Eastney Pumping Station

Was built to deal with the sewage of Portsmouth and any possible flood waters. Prior to that the sewage gathered in pits in Fort Cumberland nearby. This was offensive to the Marines living there. They were moved to Eastney Barracks and French prisoners moved in Several outbreaks of cholera due to bad drainage and an inadequate water supply happened in Portsmouth. In 1848 the Public Health Act required a water supply and drainage to be provided by the local authorities. This borough was not too quick to provide this. In 1868 sewers had been built with a high gravity system and a low level system. Both discharged untreated sewage into the harbour. In 1868 two Clayton Beam Engines and pumps were erected to provide power. These worked until 1923. With the growth of the town two Bolton and Watt beam engines and pumps were added in 1886. The sewage was then held in storage tanks and discharged into the outgoing tide. This continued until 1954. These engines can still be seen by visitors. the ever growing demand led to a new pumping house in 1904. This had gas-fired engines driving Tangye pumps. The station actually has several buildings. The first is the Clayton Engine House built in 1868, the second is the James Watt Beam Engine house of 1886. Then there is the cooling pond where the water is pumped in and out. Fourthly is the Crossley Gas Engine House of 1902. Then the Electric Motor Houses of 1922 and 1937.

Eastney Pumping Station

Memories

"My name is David Stanley, I was born on September the 24th at 6am at 46 Lindley Avenue, Eastney. The midwife was Nurse Bampton. My grandmother, Mrs Jean Joseph kept a boarding at No 4 Eastern Terrace, St Georges Road and I later lived with her and revelled in the fact that Eastney Beach was only 150 yards away. During the blitz our air raid shelter was on Eastney Front. In its time it served as the 'Sun Huts Café' and the last time I saw it was the surf shop. I went to Reginald Road School, Haslemere, Milton and Eastney Modern Schools. My class teacher at Reginald Road was Miss Redding and my contempories were Tony Hunt, the fishmongers son at Highland Road, Garth Woodhead, Brian Knox, Peter Gough and Mary Cook. I can recall street traders from that era: knife grinders, muffin man, and a barrel organ complete with monkey. The Café next door to our house originally was no more than a wooden shack with a lift up flap. Customers sat on high stools exposed to the elements. Mr and Mrs Allen were the proprietors. They retired some years ago, but I believe that Mr Allen is still alive in the west country somewhere. Next door to the café was a small commercial garage. I had to take the battery from our radio there to have it topped up - it cost sixpence. The nearest grocer was at the bottom of Adair Road. It had a vegetable department at the side and once I got into serious trouble taking empty lemonade bottles from the fruit and veg part around into the shop to claim the two pence on each bottle. On Saturday morning I would go to the Odeon Club at Southsea. It cost sixpence to get in at 9am. We had to sing songs first. Can you imagine 9 year old kids today singing 'Peg O' My Heart' and 'Tipperary'. When it was your birthday, the Manager sent you a card, which entitled you and a friend any two seats in the house.

Saturday afternoons in the winter would be spent in the 'bug hutch' that's the soubriquet for the Gaiety Cinema. In summer it was always Eastney Beach, especially for the end of the pier firework displays on summer nights.

I remember the illuminations going up after the war. Two fighting cats complete with stars that actually simulated the movement fascinated me. In those days Southsea and Eastney beach were packed. I could hear Welsh miners wives talking in Welsh as they sat on the prom and there was scarcely room to sit on the beach itself. Harry Secombe starring at South Parade Pier, Arthur English or the Band of the Royal Marines. Talent Competitions at the end of the pier and grand balls in the ballroom. Now its all plastic and slot machines.

On selected nights, a trolley bus illuminated with hundreds of light bulbs used to come along the Highland Road route. It passed the Empire Café, the Bluebird Sweetshop, Mr Fox the barber, the co-op at the top of Kimberley Road, Timothy White and Taylors and on past the cemetery.

Sunday mornings I would be parked in the shell garden of the Eastney Tavern. It was decorated with thousands of sea-shells and broken crockery, and boasted a mini zoo with monkeys and birds in cages. My mother went to the Royal Marine Sergeants Mess on Sunday nights. They played tombola or else had dances. For my sins I roamed the barracks as a boy and the Marines called us the Eastney Arabs, and showered us with sweets. I later joined the cadets under Colour Sgt Taylor and the cadet band performed at many important Portsmouth functions. My father was a serving sailor and my friend's father was on the Mauritania. All of us had something to do with the sea, so later on I joined up and went through Shotley Point at Whale Island. My great uncle was Chief G.I. there and is buried on the island. I was christened out of the Ship's bell on the quarterdeck. My first ship was Portsmouth based - HMS Armada in 1958, a battle class destroyer and even after all these years I am still in touch with about twenty of that crew. We sailed for the Med in September 1958 and spent most of our time on Cyprus Patrol.

I joined the Somerset Police Force in 1968 and live in a small village, Ditcheat, near Castle Cary. I still look back on my childhood at Eastney, despite rationing and post war austerity it was a happy time. The characters were legion. An old gent ran a sweetshop in the rank of shops opposite the bus depot. He always wore a Homburg hat and grey fingerless gloves. The shop smelt of cats and he wrote out signs on cardboard, advertising his goods. The only trouble was everything was labelled 'gorgeous' - gorgeous chocolates, or gorgeous sweets, 'cheaper than Jimmy Woolworths'. The window cleaner was Mr Dixon. He had a limp from the First World War and always left the kids on his round a lead soldier. Wish I had kept them, I would be rich now!"

"My name is Cyril Stares and I started life in Delamare Road. It was the 31st of May 1905. We moved to Landguard Road, which had a clean end and a dirty one, where the rough element lived. I went to Eastney Road School and enjoyed woodwork, which was useful later on. I still have a Coronation Cup of 1911. We moved to Suffolk Road in 1914 and I went to Milton School in Eastney Road. In 1916 I went to Wimborne Road School. My father, being a policeman, and rather strict, got permission for me to leave, just being thirteen and two weeks. He grew vegetables on an allotment and I took them round in a wheelbarrow for sale. Then I helped on a milk round for Mrs O'Brian. I went to Handleys as a van boy then a garage boy. My first driving licence was in 1922, which I still have. I saw Mr Handley a lot at work, then his three sons came back from the war. A sovereign was given to me as a war bonus. I left in 1926 to be a lorry driver for Streets the dairy of Duncan Road as mentioned in the local paper. Then I went to Parks the removers of Haslemere Road for eleven years. I was a bus driver for two years until my eyesight forced me to give it up in 1946. The S.E.B. gave me a job working in their garage, for twenty two years, until I retired. My wife and I moved to Station Road, Drayton before the war started. It was countryside then.

There was a field where Devonshire Avenue is now, with cows from Francis Avenue Dairy. There was a Prince Albert Street which is now the end of Prince Albert Road, with Hansons the grocers, Kent the drapers, and Luxton the butchers. Near Methuen Road were some small houses with front steps. In Highland Road was Seals the pork butchers. When I was three, I got lost and they sat me in the window. There was Steels Timber Yard at the back of Highland Road shops and it was burnt out in 1920. In Adair Road was a cake shop we bought yeast from. Butlers Cycle Shop has been there a long time There were three pony and traps to take people down Henderson Road to the Hayling Ferry. A large brickfield used to be between Bransbury Road and Henderson Road. Fordingbridge Road was built in 1920. Gritanwood Road was possibly named after the builder.

Bransbury Park was built on rubble. I remember the sweet factory behind the Regal being Hostlers There was a dance hall in Eastney Road where the garage is now. Only two cars seemed to be in Eastney - a Marine's and a doctor's. There was a steamroller also, parked at Eastney Pumping Station.

Whilst I was at Milton School, the headmaster was 'Boss' Allan. There were two other teachers I remember - 'Ginger' Broadbridge and 'Snowy' White."

"My name is Reginald Foyle and I have lived in Essex Road for 53 years. I started in Regent Street which has disappeared now, going to Albert Road School. My work has varied from the French Café, Albert Road, Timothy White & Taylor; Phillips the Optician, Sid Cooper the Butcher, then I went to live in Chichester, to work for the Council, cycling from Clanfield, then I worked for Costain the builders. After a while I went to work for Bucket the builder. Then I helped to build the Odeon Cinema at Southsea for Privetts. After that I worked in the Dockyard. When the war came, I joined the Royal Pioneer Corps, and moved to the Royal Engineers. Coming out, I worked for Portsmouth City Council as rodent remover. I had done this before in a small way at Dock Mill. When I was a boy, with others, the boss gave us a farthing for each rat we killed there. I went on the buses then, being a conductor for fifteen years. Finally I went back to the Dockyard as a slinger and in the Records Office. I remember the sweet factory called Lathers behind the Regal Cinema. Turners used to be the Bransbury Café and the Black Hut run by Jim Borer. Stokes Cycle shop in Eastney Road, Brays the Chemist now Heron Davis. A pub named Barracks Cellars used to be on the corner of Henderson Road, now both the corner and the pub have gone. There was a man with a horse and cart used to take people to Hayling Ferry. Sometimes he would leave his beer to drink when he returned. One day his glass was left a long time, and his body was discovered outside in the cart. His faithful horse had brought him back.

I remember a duckpond in Bransbury Road and a house made of metal sheets. The Glory Hole used to be a duck pond with water and crabs, etc. We boys used to dig for bullets at Fort Cumberland to use as fishing weights and other things. There used to be six cottages where Cumberland Tavern is now. These were torn down to build the pub, which is now being made into flats.

I remember Prince Albert Road with Baights Shoe Shop opposite Economy Grocers, corner of Landguard Road, butchers, a fish and chip shop and Yorkies corner shop. Stonehams corner of Suffolk Road. They were shoe repairers etc. Atkin the printers. Woodmancote Road corner had Buxeys Newsagent. Manship the Grocer is now a self-drive office. A greengrocer on the corner of Essex Road is now a fish and chip shop. Hellyers the grocers and 107 Prince Albert Road was Borer the greengrocer. Fords sweetshop was a butchers. The Shepherd's Crook pub used to be on the opposite corner in Priory Crescent. Some remains of the old canal could be seen in the Goldsmith Avenue. When I was six years old I was taken by Mr Fox to hospital in his horse drawn ambulance in 1918. A family named Cleverley had a horse-drawn bus service and brought 'Dockies' to work from the country. I remember Baffins Road being built in 1926. The truck I was on, delivering for Timothy White & Taylors got stuck in the mud and we needed help from the workmen."

"Geographically Eastney has seen many changes since my childhood days. The trams ran in a semi-circle round the town, beginning at Eastney and ending at Milton, leaving Eastney Road devoid of public transport and eventually lines were laid joining the two points and creating a circular route. With wheeled traffic beginning to increase the road at the end of Eastney and Highland Road was widened - a public house and adjacent fresh fish shops were razed, thereby increasing the access to Henderson and Cromwell Road, while on the opposite side of the main road between the mission church at the end of Methuen Road and the Highland Arms public house a row of cottages was razed and the pavement at the front of the pub narrowed. The Mayflower public house, once olde worlde cottage with front gardens stood back from the main road. The long gardens at the back merged with the gardens at the back of Methuen Road as did the shops in Highland Road leading to Prince Albert Street and were divided by a corrugated iron fence. Between the area there was a large house with adjacent hand laundry, a pawnbroker, two cottages, a timber merchant, pork butcher, dairy, greengrocer and draper. On the opposite side a butcher, chemist, grocer, hardware, baker, shoe shop, post office, paper shop and a shop selling anything from pins to toys and patent medicines, a greengrocer cum coal merchant, who in the summer, owning a horse and trap carrying six people, plied from the end of Henderson Road to Hayling Island Ferry - the crossing made by rowing boat during the summer months, and on the corner of Cromwell Road a sweetshop. As bus travel increased it was decided by the City Council that a bus garage was needed in the south to augment the one at North End. Part of the long gardens in Highland Road adjoining the back of the gardens in Methuen Road were purchased and a garage erected with the entrance at Eastney Terminus through to Prince Albert Street. With a prevailing wind the height of the building caused a down-draught in the houses in Methuen Road with smoke and soot blowing out of the coal burning fires - electricity was yet to come and it meant the inhabitants having to purchase alternative heating. There were protest meetings but no redress. Now with private motoring the building has become redundant. A farm at the top of Henderson Road and stretching to Bransbury Road was bought by the council for the erection of houses for families on limited income, with tenants taking a pride in their well tended gardens. I can remember the cul de sac at the top end of Eastney Farm Road as a duck pond - now filled in and a bed of roses taking its place. The park on the opposite side of the road was once a morass. Prior to being drained some gypsies once set up a fairground with adjacent caravans and chickens and ducks - it was prior to television and proved quite popular, but the heavy machinery driving the roundabout sank into the boggy soil and outside help was needed to pull it out. Bransbury Park is now an asset to the district with flower beds on well kept lawns with garden seats, a sport area, a children's playground and a large Community Centre catering for various interests."

Queenie Trace

"I was born on the 23rd of November, 1923 in my grandmother's front bedroom at 5 Essex Road, Milton, directly opposite the now demolished Eastney Police Station. As I wasn't expected to live more than a few days I was christened in that room by the vicar of St James's Church, by the same vicar who married my parents 12 months previous.

Both my parents had been raised in the Eastney district, had been childhood sweethearts and had attended the same school, Milton School on the corner of Dunbar and Eastney Roads. It seemed strange that a few years later I also attended that school and in my formative years was taught by the same teacher who taught my parents, a Miss Barnett who lived with her mother and sister at 11 St George's Road. The sister was also a teacher but more of that later.

My father, who up to the time of his marriage to mother lived at 77 Eastney Road with his parents, five brothers and a sister although after serving in the Royal Field Artillery in Mesopotamia (now Iraq and Iran) he joined the Royal Irish Constabulary in 1918 but had to leave in 1922 when the Irish Free State came into being as did Ulster. During that period he won the King's Police Medal for gallantry when he rescued a sergeant and ten constables from an ambush laid by the I.R.A. Although he was only fourteen years of age when he joined up he put four years on his age in order to join up. But then that was the expected thing in those days. His father was an Armoury Sergeant in the Royal Garrison Artillery whilst my mother's father was the Regimental Sergeant Major both serving in the same regiment then occupying Southsea Castle.

On leaving the Irish Force he sunk all his pension commutation into a small shop called the "Chocolate Box" at 88 Upper Church Path, Landport. Unfortunately it was the wrong time to go into business with the great depression of the 20's about to descend and he had to give it up owing quite a bit of money to wholesalers (which, I hasten to add he paid back every penny owed) and we moved into one room at 17 Reginald Road, Eastney. In that room my parents, my younger brother and myself ate and slept and in fact my eldest sister was born in the room. They were terrible times. The owner of the property was a Mr George Black who lived there with his wife and his father in law and they led us a dog's life. Mrs Black had a very mean and frightening streak in her as she often hid in the dark passageway at the foot of the stairs leading from the main passageway and jumped out on my brother and self putting the "fear of God" into us.

At that time I attended Reginald Road School where I was taught by the other Miss Barnett, the sister to the teacher at Milton Road School. They were very much alike in appearance even to the buns at the back of their hair styles, the hats and the very clothing they wore. Both sisters believed in the old maxim "Spare the rod and you spoil the child". Both were extremely strict in their classrooms which they ruled with a rod of iron and also in the respective playgrounds during break time. Their voices could be heard all over the schools in which they taught.

In those days Reginald Road School had a foundry and a kind of blacksmith's forge where all kinds of metal and tin work was taught. Meon Road School held the woodworking classes and it was indeed a pleasure to attend at either school to be taught the rudiments of a trade.

In 1929 my father obtained employment with the Royal Automobile Club who had obtained a 10 years contract with the Watch Committee of Portsmouth to man all major road junctions in the City. I can well remember him performing his traffic control duties at the Strand, Southsea, South Parade Pier, Palmerston Road, North End and Northern Road, Cosham where he was knocked down and severely injured by a sailor who had taken a "joy-ride" on a motorcycle which he had stolen from the Dockyard - so you see that sort of misdemeanour went on even in those far off days!. He was on duty in the Guildhall Square when World War II was declared.

In the 20's and 30's there was no such organisation as the National Health Service and if the services of a doctor were required and he attended your home then his fee was 2/6d, 12½p in todays money.

Actually I am getting slightly ahead of myself because in 1930 our family moved into 3 rooms at number 77 Eastney Road which was the home of my paternal grandmother - grandfather Wallace having left her many years previously and who had passed away in 1927 in Prince George Street, Portsea. It was in that year that I transferred from Reginald Road School to Milton Road School (although it was really Eastney Road).

In those days the trams rumbled past the house either on their normal route or on their way back to the depot at Eastney which stood at the junction of Highland and Eastney Roads next door to what was then Eastney Gospel Mission.

Every morning at 6am we were roused from our slumbers by the sound of "Reveille" emanating from the Royal Marine Barracks at Eastney in Cromwell Road. On a Sunday morning the Royals would attend Church Parade at St.

Andrew's Church, Henderson Road and at the conclusion of the same they would march back to barracks via Henderson and Bransbury Roads, into Eastney Road past our house and back into Cromwell Road and the Barracks. Looking back in time it was an occasion for we lads who marched alongside them on pavements the whole contingent being played back by their band.

Around 1934 in the summer months the Locks at the top of Locksway Road became a happy playground for we boys. The remains of the Arundel to Portsmouth Canal extended from the foreshore to where Waterlock Gardens is now situated and there were a number of abandoned boats lying on the mud in the canal. These were ideal for us to go climbing around on and searching for crabs. Many a time on coming out of Milton School at 4pm I, along with other school chums would go direct to the canal instead of going home and play up there and not go home until darkness descended only to find we had been reported to the police at Eastney Police Station as "missing from home". Of course my father would give me a hiding and send me up to bed without any tea (this would be smuggled up later by my mother!). It didn't make any difference, the pull of the canal was too strong. In later years when I joined the Portsmouth City Police I found myself stationed at Eastney Police Station and I came across an old "Occurrence Book" for that period and found my name etc. written down there by one Constable Bob Egerton as a boy missing from home and who had later returned home and had been suitably chastised by a parent!

At that period whilst at Milton School I can often recall crossing the road to visit my grandmother Miles at 5 Essex Road and pausing a while to stand on tip-toe to peer into the fire station at the back of the police station and wonder in awe at the huge red and brassy fire engine garaged there. Little did I know that in August 1939 as a police cadet attached to the Portsmouth City Police Fire Brigade, stationed at the Central Fire Station in Park Road (now King Henry I Road) that I would be cleaning the brass on that same engine which was now housed in the police ambulance shed on the corner of Nelson Square and Park Road (where the automatic telephone exchange is now situated). Incidentally part of the old Fire Station can be seen opposite the Guildhall. The doors have been bricked up as had the window of the Watchroom but they are clearly visible. Memory also takes me back to Fort Cumberland, then in the occupation of the Royal Marines. Alongside the beach in that area where now stands the defunct Fraser Battery were the rifle ranges for the Royals with a huge "butt" dominating the area and from which the targets were raised and lowered. When firing was taking place a red flag was flown at the back of where the public toilets are now situated and also from a flag pole on the beach. The Royals section of Eastney beach was barred to the public by the means of a line of wooden posts reaching down to the sea from those toilets and there was always a Marine Stick sentry on duty to prevent any incursion. Our job was to evade him and the Royal Marine Police who had a walking guard on the butts and dive among the sand at the butts and retrieve the lead bullets which had been fired at the targets raised there. If we were ever caught, and it wasn't very often, we would get the customary clip around the ear and sent packing. Nowadays if that sort of thing had still been in being, the local constabulary and the Juvenile Court and Probation Officers would be involved! How times have changed. The Glory Hole was another place frequented by we lads. This was the name given to a small bay off Eastney Lake. Hayling Ferry Road ran alongside it and there was a small bridge crossing its entrance. It was here that the Admiralty, as the M.O.D. (Navy) was then called, dumped a great deal of its rubbish from its ships, the dockyard, the Naval Barracks in Edinburgh Road and the Marines Barracks at Eastney. We often played there coming home with old discarded Marine pith helmets, bayonets (which were promptly taken from us by our parents) and other paraphenalia. No thought was ever given to problems now being raised concerning asbestos etc.

Municipal and Parliamentary election time brought forth our little "gangs" of boys all supporting various local candidates with their photos nailed to long pieces of wood which would be raised aloft as we marched around the area singing the praises of "our" candidate "Vote, vote, vote for Mr......., whose that knocking at your door? If you don't let him in you'll get punched under the chin, and you won't go voting any more!" These chants often led to war with other boys doing the same for their candidate - black eyes etc being the order of the day! As I recall it the streets were not all that well lit, gas lighting still being the prevalent lighting for side streets and some main roads. The fun seems to have departed electioneering these days.

My father was a great Do It Yourself expert. In the early 30's, somewhere around 1931/32, in the days when a wireless consisted of a cat's whisker and earphones, my father decided to try his hand at making a wireless with a loudspeaker attached. Battery and accumulator sets were just becoming the in thing and so our neighbour, (a Mr Hale who was a tram driver and a T.A. soldier) and my father got their heads together in our one living room and built the set on our one and only table. My father made the ornate cabinet from 3-ply wood and after many false alarms, wonders upon wonders we could sit and listen to music and plays. Most of the equipment used in the radio was purchased from a partnership formed by the late Laurie Threadingham and his partner, K Jerome. During the day these gentlemen ran a thriving window cleaning business but in the evenings they operated a small radio business from a garage in Landguard Road at the rear of Blaenavon Stores on the corner of Landguard and Eastney Roads. The store was a grocery store run by a Mr & Mrs Flemming. Mr Flemming had only one leg and we understood he had lost it in the Boer War. Later the partnership broke up, Laurie Threadingham opening up several radio shops in the Eastney and Milton Districts which he later passed on to his sons. Mr Jerome also opened up similar shops at Gosport and Tangier Road, Copnor.

Near 88 few doors away was a second hand book shop owned by a Mr

Montague who was also the commissionaire at the Eastney Electric Cinema (later to become the Regal Cinema) on the corner of Devonshire Avenue and Eastney Road. He was an ex Royal Navy man and my last memories of him was as an Admiralty Police Constable serving in the Portsmouth Dockyard sometime in the 50's.

Several of the houses on this side of the road had been built as flats. The spiral staircases at the front of the buildings made ideal places for we lads to play at cowboys etc and hiding in the spaces under the stairs. Our antics often brought wrath upon our heads from the occupants of the lower flats who were fed up with the noises we created.

Prior to moving into the Reginald Road address (the same being demolished by a bomb during World War II) my father had obtained employment working on the new railway station at Wimbledon and once a month he would cycle back to our sweet shop in Upper Church Path, Landport on a Friday night and return the following Sunday afternoon. That cycle earned an honourable retirement when we moved into number 77 Eastney Road and it was hung on the wall of my Grandmother's shed.

For a saddle he had utilised an old motor cycle saddle and I should think he must have appreciated its comfort too as these journeys were done before the road over Butser Hill had been levelled down.

Also in the car park of the cinema was a very large tin hut which housed a sweet factory of Scarlett and Layther and to which we kids "homed" in after school and on our various ways

home. There were always cardboard boxes left outside the hut and upon investigation could be found the odd sweet or two. Mind you we had to dodge the occasional clip around the ear if caught by an employee.

In the 1920's and 1930's no ball games were allowed in Milton Park only in Bransbury Park and if the park keeper saw you kicking a ball around you were sent packing. Milton Park had quite a large bandstand in its centre where local dance groups gave public displays. It was always a good early evenings entertainment to be taken there by mother, never father, and watch or listen to a band etc. Bransbury Park held an area which contained free slides, merry-go-rounds and suchlike and which were fully used by we kids. In those days the ground on which the fun fair stood was hard gravel and we often returned home with deep cuts and grazes on our knees and legs.

When I first went to Milton School in 1930 the teachers were Miss Barnett, Mr Hinks (whom I still see around and natter to), Mr Hare and Mr Blundell (both of whom later moved to Meon Road School), Mr Lovelock, Mr Cooper, Mr Scarlett and Mr Sperring. Mr Sperring was a naturalist/botanist and often took boys to Farlington marshes to catch butterflies and tadpoles as well as newts etc., for the class aquariums. Mr Scarlett was in charge of the "bright" boys who were to take the annual examination for the entry into the Southern Secondary School then in Fawcett Road which later became the Southern

Grammar School for Boys before moving to Baffins. Mr Lovelock took the school football team. During my time there we had two headmasters, a Mr Williams and later Mr Young."

❖ ❖ ❖ ❖ ❖ ❖ ❖ ❖

This booklet was compiled by the members of the W.E.A. Local History Group which meets at the Bucland Community Centre, Malins Road, North End, Portsmouth. The group is made up of local people who wish to record the history of ordinary peoples' lives and the streets in which they live. The group is very informal and welcomes new members who care to come to Malins Road on a Tuesday evening during term time or write to us.

Class Members:

Leonard Bufton, Anton Cox, Sandy Ellerton, Betty Fowkes, Peter Galvin, Malcolm Garlick (Sketches), Kevin Goldring, Pat Goldring, Charles Hutchins, Stephen Pomeroy (Chairman & Editor), Chris Redgrave, Jeff Smith, Rita Wall and Margaret Webster (Treasurer).

Honorary Members:

Don Miles (Typesetting), Olive Cook (Proof Reader).

Affiliated Members:

Des Beaumont, Morecambe, Lancashire
Vic Burly, Brisbane, Australia
Maggie Munro, Frankstone, Australia

Contributors:

Wally, Leslie Bern, Harold Lewis, Reginald Foyle, Robin Phillips, Charlie Renyard, Evelyn Savage, David Stanley, Cyril Stares, Queenie Trace, Edith Turner, Eddie Wallace.

© 1994

First published in 1994.
Reprinted in 2010

WEA (Portsmouth Branch Local History Group)
Adult Education Centre
Buckland Community Centre
Malins Road, North End,
Portsmouth

ISBN 987-1-873911-04-4